PAUL'S
PRISON PRAYERS

PAUL'S PRISON PRAYERS

by

W. Graham Scroggie

KREGEL PUBLICATIONS
Grand Rapids, MI 49501

Paul's Prison Prayers by W. Graham Scroggie.
Published by Kregel Publications
a division of Kregel, Inc. All rights reserved.

Library of Congress Cataloging in Publication Data

Scroggie, William Graham, 1877-1958.
   Paul's Prison Prayers.

   Reprint of the 1921 ed. published by Pickering &
Inglis, London.
   1. Bible — Prayers — Addresses, essays, lectures.
2. Paul, Saint, apostle — Addresses, essays, lectures.
I. Title.
BV235.S35   1981   242'.5   80-8077
ISBN 0-8254-3737-7 (pbk.)

Printed in the United States of America

CONTENTS

FOREWORD

IN the hope that the four Prayers here so inadequately treated, may be abundantly answered in the experience of the reader, and that we all may be led to a further and fuller study of these noble utterances, this unpretentious volume is sent forth.

May Divine Knowledge, and Wisdom, and Love, and Power, be the increasing portion of us all who name that Name.

W. GRAHAM SCROGGIE

And this I pray, that your love may abound yet more and more in knowledge and in all judgment;

That ye may approve things that are excellent; that ye may be sincere and without offence till the day of Christ;

Being filled with the fruits of righteousness, which are by Jesus Christ unto the glory and praise of God.

Philippians 1:9-11

1

PRAYER FOR DISCERNING LOVE

IT is important to see the connection of the verses of this prayer with what immediately precedes. In verses 3 to 7, with the Philippian converts in view, the Apostle has been giving praise for their progress. Then he at once turns to prayer for their perfecting in verses 9 to 11, and the two paragraphs are united by verse 8, where confident hope and anxious prayer meet in human longing towards them, and the day of Christ, which is the goal of his expectation, is also the terminus of his intercession; not till then will either his hopes be finally fulfilled, or his fears finally suppressed. There must be no rest, he would teach us, in what is attained. Our prosperity is to be measured not so much by the point we have reached as by the fact and measure of the progress we are making. 'Speak ye unto the children of Israel that they go forward.' There is room for it; there is need of it; there is a call to it; and there is blessedness in it. Exhibiting that tact for which he prays, Paul thanks first, and supplicates after. He first encourages his converts, and then he intercedes for them. The very occasion for praise makes prayer necessary, lest we be so occupied with the actual as to lose the vision of the possible. We must ever remember the petty done and the vast undone; the petty attained and accomplished, and what yet remains to be accomplished and attained. The Apostle sets before us, as the ideal, perfect character in the world, and in order to an ever closer approximation to this he discloses the regulating principle in the heart. This is *love*. 'I pray that your love.' In that word the keynote of the prayer is struck. This is not the love of mere desire, sentiment, or emotion, but the outgoing of the entire nature in self-sacrificing service. It is the sympathy of the heart, and the devotion of the life to its object, and as such it is the supreme proof of the reality of our Christian profession. Love possessed must be expressed not only toward God but toward man, and it is the latter for which the Apostle here prays.

Taking, then, the possession and exhibition of discerning love to be the subject of this prayer, let us observe that for its realisation the process of its perfecting is first of all unfolded; the purpose of its perfecting is then displayed; and, finally, the power of its perfecting is revealed. Under cover of these simple divisions the prayer will open up to us its treasured store. We shall take it clause by clause, and as far as possible word by word; drawing inspiration from the exposition; and let us never forget that inspiration which does not rest on exposition will sooner or later pass away. We need a firm ground of truth for Christian emotion, or it is bound to evaporate. So let us then consider these parts of the prayer.

First of all,

I.—THE NECESSARY PROCESS OF LOVE'S PERFECTING IS UNFOLDED

'I pray that your love may abound yet more and more in knowledge and all discernment for you to test things that differ.' Here are three distinct movements of thought, setting before us, first, the enlargement, second, the enrichment, and, finally, the employment of our love.

The Enlargement of Love (the first clause of verse 9): 'I pray that your love may abound yet more and more.' The thought of *Plenitude* at once presents itself in the words, 'may abound.' With its cognates, it occurs in the New Testament about ninety times; and, as distinguished from the idea of sufficiency, it connotes *superfluity, beyond measure, enough and to spare*. Hence that significant utterance in 2 Cor. ix. 8, 'God is able to make to abound toward you all grace; so that ye always having all sufficiency'—mark the change of the word—'in all things, may abound'—back to the first word again—'unto every good work.' In that passage the sufficiency is fulness for ourselves; but the abundance is overflowing for others; and others are blessed truly and permanently only by our overflow. Paul revels in the thought of spiritual growth and overflow, and desires this especially in respect of love.

But there is, further, the thought of *Progress*. 'Yet more and more.' Here is a generous recognition of the exercise of love on the part of these Philippians. But there is a hint also of its deficiency. There were misunderstandings in the Church, resulting in a want of unity; and this fact underlies much that the Apostle says, until he plainly speaks of it in chapter iv. verse 2. Grateful for that measure of grace which they already possessed, he desires that it should be ever more and more. The present good must always be the beginning only of something better.

Still further, in this pregnant clause there is the

thought of *Persistence*—not only plenitude and progress, but persistence. The tense indicates that the process is continuous. Growth, of which the New Testament speaks so much, is the law of life. There must therefore be not only advancement, but development, and development at every stage and from day to day. Thus in the so rich desire of the Apostle two ideas unite— the idea of fulness and the idea of progress; fulness up to the limit of capacity, and movement forward in that state of fulness all the time; state and growth; abounding and advancing; flowing in and flowing over. 'I pray that your love may abound yet more and more.'

The Apostle calls our attention, in the next place, to the *Enrichment of Love* in the words, 'in knowledge and all discernment.' The thought here is not that knowledge and discernment are the spheres in which love is to increase. but that increase of love is to be by increase of knowledge and discernment. Love is a gift from God, but in its human aspect it is a grace which must be based upon knowledge and strengthened by use. If it is to abound yet more and more, it must be fed by truth and diligently practised. I need hardly say, surely, that love may be both ignorant and foolish. But knowledge will correct the ignorance, and discernment will correct the folly.

It will be well for us to understand the nature of the qualities that are here needed and sought. *Knowledge* and *discernment*. Again and again the Apostle strikes this note of *knowledge*, by which he means not intellectual ability, which is altogether independent of love, but spiritual insight; not theoretical apprehension of truth by the mind, but a knowledge that is at once advanced, exact, full, spiritual, and experimental. It is spiritual knowledge partly as being bound up with our spiritual nature and needs, partly and chiefly as being imparted by the Holy Spirit, through Whose influence alone the truth, in the fullest and deepest sense of the word, can be known. But it is knowledge in the strictest sense of the word, for it is imparted and acquired through the sanctified understanding. We do not generally associate love and knowledge. Yet, as Christ is the Substance of all truth, as well as the Object of all love, as we love Him we shall come to know Him, and as we know Him we shall love Him. It may be necessary for us sometimes to remind ourselves that ignorance is not the hall-mark of spirituality, and while this and kindred passages do not exalt intellectuality, they do promote intelligence.

The other quality to which reference is made is *discernment*, by which is meant sensitiveness of perception through the exercise of the faculty, quickness of ethical tact. Love is not to be a blind and sentimental emotion, but is to act in conjunction with our faculty of 'judgment' or practical insight. The word occurs here only in the New Testament, and stands for 'that delicate tact and instinct which almost intuitively perceives what is right, and almost unconsciously shrinks from what is wrong. Our love must be trained to be itself a universal spiritual sense, at once the eye and the ear and the hand of the heart, seeing and hearing and touching in things Divine, with a sure and delicate feeling that seldom needs correction.' This faculty, which we exercise with reference to art and music, finds its noblest use in the realm of the moral and the spiritual. But the possession of this grace is the result only of sedulous culture and use; it will not just come. It is characteristic only of the mature; of those, as the writer to the Hebrews says, who 'by reason of habit, have their senses exercised to discern both good and evil.'

The most striking illustration in the Bible of discerning love is found in 1 Corinthians xiii. This Hymn to Love is little more than the praise of its marvellous discrimination, and reveals how manifold are the demands for its exercise. There is no perfection in this world short of full realisation of 1 Corinthians xiii. And the manifoldness of the demands for the exercise of discernment is reflected in our passage, in the word 'all,' which means every kind of discernment, discernment in every direction, all the time, and with reference to all things.

We are now in a position to understand the relation of these qualities of *knowledge* and *discernment* to one another. 'I pray that your love may abound yet more and more in knowledge and all discernment.' Why does the Apostle here unite these two qualities? We may say that knowledge is general, discernment is particular; knowledge is intelligence, discernment is intuition; knowledge deals with principles, discernment is concerned with applications. In knowledge is the idea of receptivity, but in discernment the idea of perceptivity. Knowledge is the apprehension of the truth; discernment is the exercise of tact. Knowledge makes discernment possible; and discernment makes knowledge practical. 'I pray that your love may abound yet more and more in knowledge and all discernment'; and what God hath joined together let no man put asunder.

When we consider the work of these qualities in relation to love, we see at once that they are protective and stimulative. They safeguard love on the one hand,

and they assist it on the other hand. In order to attain perfection love needs to be brought under the influence of truth. Ignorant love can be very cruel, and always tends to be erratic, seeking worthy objects in unworthy ways. But knowledge and discernment will safeguard and assist love, and by these must love be fed, and regulated and preserved. In this way, then, love is at once enriched and enriching. It is enriched as it becomes evermore intelligent and discerning; and thus, in turn, it is enriching in that it is more potent in its influence and operation. Love, therefore, is to be enlarged, is to abound yet more and more; and as it is enlarged it is to be enriched by knowledge and discernment. What for?

The next clause tells us what is the *Employment of Love:* 'That ye may approve the things that are excellent.' This clause may also be rendered, 'That ye may test things that differ.' As these thoughts are vitally related, we shall suppose that both are intended, and combine them thus:—'For you to prove the things that differ, so that you may approve the things that are excellent.' Neither one nor the other of these ideas exhausts the passage. The one, 'approving the things that are excellent,' results from the other. There is no true *approving* where there has not first been a *proving*.

What has preceded is a qualification for what now follows. The growth of love in knowledge and discernment is with a view to action. And here three matters of immense importance emerge. There is, first of all, a recognition of distinctions—'things that differ.' We might do worse than have that in the form of a motto in our rooms, particularly in our studies— 'Things that differ.' It is to be feared that there is a widespread tendency in our time to obliterate distinctions, to erase straight lines of demarcation. Many Christians are living in the borderland of things doubtful, alike in thought and in practice. Others do not recognise as they should the clear-cut distinctions everywhere present in the New Testament between right and wrong, truth and error, light and darkness, life and death. We are suffering much from a lack of definition. Theology must never be made colourless in the interests of charity, nor lax conduct be extenuated on the ground of infirmity. There are things that differ, and it is the function of a well-informed and discriminating love to observe them.

But, it may be asked, how is this recognition of distinction to be arrived at? The answer is, by an examination of qualities. We are to prove or test things to form a judgment as to their quality. Such a rich endowment as verse 9 represents is not necessary in order to discriminate between what is good and what is bad. We can do that without any special keenness of discrimination, or any deep, profound knowledge. This examination, therefore, must be of different shades of goodness, gradations of worthiness, successive ranks of spiritual merit. It is the good that too often robs us of the better; and it is the better, alas! that holds us back from the best. But for the exercise of this discrimination, training is necessary—the training not of intellect, but of love. I am not despising intellect, I am simply keeping to the text. Love will listen with discernment to life's music; love will look with discernment on life's beauty; love will touch with discernment life's qualities, so as to know what is true, and pure, and just, and good, from all possible counterfeits and distortions. This discernment is specially needful to-day, when many views and voices are apt to distract and lead astray, and when love itself, in proportion to its enthusiasm, may sadly err if divorced from the enriching and regulating qualities of knowledge and discernment.

Furthermore, this passage teaches us that this recognition of distinctions and this examination of qualities has in view an approbation of excellencies. 'That ye may approve.' Knowledge and perception will lead to choice. Neither is to be merely speculative. We are to prove in order to approve; we are to discover the better way in order to pursue it. 'And yet show I unto you a more excellent way.' Bringing enlightened judgment to bear on influences, opinions and courses of conduct, has for its only proper end choosing the good and refusing the evil, choosing the better in preference to the good, and choosing the best in preference to the better. How sad a possibility it is to discern the better and yet to choose the worse.

> God has His best things for the few,
>   Who dare to stand the test;
> God has His second choice for those,
>   Who will not have His best.

That second choice is sure to be good, but it will never be any compensation for the loss of the best. Let us learn, therefore, that we must bring an intelligent and discerning love to bear upon the whole economy and order of life, to exhibit at every turn, 'the sacred cunning of enlightened love, receiving and using with more and more skilful care and careful skill those infallible monitions of the Holy Spirit, Whose elect and favourite instrument within the human heart is love.' Nothing but love can enable us truly and always to distinguish things which, though outwardly similar, essentially differ. It has truly been said that 'no practical discriminations or determinations are of any worth in God's sight, except as they are animated by love, and indeed determined by it. If a Christian should choose anything, or reject anything, yet not in love, his choice as a matter of fact may be right, but for all that, the man himself is wrong.' 'I pray that your love may abound yet more and more in knowledge and all discernment, for you to test things that differ, with a view to approving the things that are excellent.' That is the necessary process, and leads us to the consideration of how

II.—The Manifold Purpose of Love's Perfecting is Displayed

'That ye may be sincere and without offence, being filled with the fruit of righteousness.' The equipment of the preceding clause is to issue in character and conduct. This rich endowment is intended for a practical and permanent effect, and this effect is to be seen in several directions. The purpose is related to God, to man, and to ourselves.

Look at *the purpose Godward*. Summarily this is *trueness of conscience*. 'That ye may be sincere.' There is much difference of opinion as to the origin of this word. But two suggested derivations are so attractive in this connection that we venture to call attention to them. The suggestion that 'sincere' comes from the Latin words meaning *without wax*, and is associated with a device, at one time, on the part of sculptors, of correcting flaws in their marble by filling up the crevices with a carefully prepared wax—an imposition which time and heat and damp would ultimately reveal. It is said that this led contractors in their agreements to bind the artist to do his work *sine cera*, or *without wax*. The other suggested derivation is that the word comes from Greek words meaning *tested by sunlight*, perhaps with an allusion to the Eastern practice of stowing away goods in dark corners of bazaars so that the customer cannot clearly see what he is buying. Whichever of these may be the origin of the word, what we commonly understand by 'sincere' is challenge enough, and, as it has to do with the motives, this will be the effect to Godward of a disciplined and growing love.

In the one view it is required of us that we be pure, genuine, real, free from all foreign elements, without hypocrisy, being what we profess and appear to be; not feigned, not simulated, not assumed; clear of all base mixtures—in short, *perfectly open towards God*.

How great is the need of such reality it is scarcely necessary to say—the need of downright genuineness and sincerity in ourselves and in others, in motive and in practice, in speech and in print, in our homes and abroad, in our bosoms and in our businesses. We would do well to pray now and always for a passion for reality. 'That ye may be sincere.' When the Church of God is transparently sincere, the things for which we are praying will be accomplished.

In the other view of the derivation of the word, the Christian should be able to stand the test of the light. His should be a life true and transparent, and characterised by sacred simplicity. What the sun is in nature, the great detector, the all-seeing face of God is in the religious life. The eye of God will be the final test, and we should live with that fact in view.

Let us remember that sincerity can be amazingly ignorant, and can do incalculable damage. As, for example, the sincerity of Saul, who, notwithstanding all his persecuting, could say, 'I have lived in all good conscience before God until this day.' Christian sincerity, the sincerity of this prayer, is not untutored, undisciplined, but is the product of an enlightened and discerning love.

Look, further, at *the purpose Manward*. Summarily this is *consistency of conduct*. 'That ye may be without offence.' This word occurs only twice in the New Testament—in Acts xxiv. 16, with an intransitive force; and in 1 Corinthians x. 32, with a transitive force. It may have either significance in our text, and although the view commonly taken is that here it means, never stumbling over a wrong motive, referring to the inward life, we prefer to take the other view—that Paul is praying that they and we may give no offence, that we may in no case lay a cause of stumbling in the way of others, that we be not stumbling-blocks, but stepping-stones. These two ideas, after all, are intimately related. The one referring to an inward condition; the other to an outward relation. Both meet in actual experience, for it is only as we are right within that our relation to others can be true. The Christian who himself stumbles is a stumbling-block. It must be therefore our ambition to have 'a conscience void of offence toward God and man.' Yet, Christian duty though it be, it may easily fail of its end. For even Christ, Who could say, 'which of you convinceth Me of sin?' had also to say, 'blessed is he whosoever shall not be offended in

Me.' The duty therefore has its necessary limitations.

What, then, is the relation of these two words to one another—'sincere,' and 'without offence'? What is prayed for is our perfection, and this, of course, has two sides—the Godward and manward; the inward and outward; character on the one hand, and conduct on the other. 'Sincere,' and 'without offence,' stand in this relation to one another—they are interdependent. One cannot hope to be offenceless who is not sincere, and one cannot be right toward God and remain wrong toward man. These, therefore, are vitally related, and both are the product of a love in process of being perfected.

But there is, further, *the purpose Selfward*. Summarily this is *fulness of character*. 'Being filled with the fruit of righteousness.' All the words in this clause are rich in suggestion and instruction. Mark the gracious product —'Fruit of righteousness.' Whether we regard righteousness as the fruit, or the fruit as the result of righteousness, does not affect the essential truth of the passage. No doubt both ideas are present. A right relation between God and man, entered into at conversion, will, under the influence of the Holy Spirit, issue in right conduct, so that righteousness is both root and fruit, cause and effect. As cause, righteousness will refer to character, and as effect it will refer to conduct. Then, observe the other word, 'fruit.' There is an almost uniform distinction made in the New Testament between *works* and *fruit*; the former pointing to service, and *fruit* to character. Therefore, here, fruit refers not to what we do, but to what we are; not to our Christian activity, but to our likeness to Christ; not to our relation to men, but to our condition of soul.

What, then, is this fruit? It is described in Galatians v. 22, 23, and the threefold relation which we have now in view is present there. The fruit is to-Godward, 'love, joy, peace.' To-manward, it is 'long-suffering, gentleness, goodness.' To-selfward, it is 'faith, meekness, self-control.' It is of these that, in John xv., we are bidden bear 'some,' more,' and 'much.'

And what is to be the wondrous measure of this grace? The answer is: '*Filled* with the fruit of righteousness.' This word has, throughout the New Testament, a meaning that it obtained on the day of Pentecost, a meaning that ought never to be softened down or explained away. It points to a fulness and richness of experience to which, alas! most of us are strangers. It leaves no room for the notion that any defect is necessary in the religious life, but is one way of affirming that we need not, and therefore should not, sin; nor shall we, if we are filled with the fruit of righteousness, filled with grace, filled unto all the fulness of God, filled with His Spirit. Only such fruit should be borne by us, and it should be borne in abundance; for the fulness of the Spirit of Christ in the Christian is without measure, according to our created capacity. Well may we sing:

> Lord, I ask it, hardly knowing
>   What this wondrous gift may be;
> But, fulfil to overflowing,
>   Thy great meaning let me see.

The purpose, therefore, of our perfecting has this threefold bearing: to-Godward, trueness of conscience; to-manward, consistency of conduct; and to-selfward, fulness of character.

III.—THE ENABLING POWER OF LOVE'S PERFECTING IS REVEALED

Of the remaining expressions in this passage there are three: 'Until the day of Christ,' 'through Jesus Christ,' and 'unto the glory and praise of God.' In the first, 'Until the day of Christ,' we get the ruling motive of such a life, in the second, 'Through Jesus Christ,' we get the Divine secret; and in the last, 'Unto the glory and praise of God,' we get the ultimate object. And so the Apostle prays that their and our love may abound yet more and more in knowledge and all discernment, so that we may test things that differ, with a view to approving the things that are excellent, in order that we may to-Godward be sincere, to-manward, offence-less, and to-selfward bear the fruit of righteousness in abundance, living in the light of Christ's certain return. He does not say we are to live such a life in view of death. Death is not a certainty, but Christ's second advent is, and in the light of Christ's return we are to live this life. And we are to live it 'through Jesus Christ,' its great secret; and we are to live it, first and last, 'unto the glory and praise of God.' May we seek, and then receive here and now, and ever, a baptism of Christian love.

For this cause we also, since the day we heard *it*, do not cease to pray for you, and to desire that ye might be filled with the knowledge of his will in all wisdom and spiritual understanding;

That ye might walk worthy of the Lord unto all pleasing, being fruitful in every good work, and increasing in the knowledge of God;

Strengthened with all might according to his glorious power, unto all patience and longsuffering with joyfulness;

Giving thanks unto the Father, Who hath made us meet to be partakers of the inheritance of the saints in light.

Colossians 1:9-12

2

PRAYER FOR ENLIGHTENED BEHAVIOR

IN the two opening clauses of Colossians i. 9-12 are summarised both the purport and the purpose of this Prayer.

It may be said to be A PRAYER FOR ENLIGHTENED BEHAVIOUR—a knowledge of God's will pointing to enlightenment, and a life lived in conformity to that will pointing to behaviour.

The remainder of the Prayer is but an elaboration of this second clause.

The Prayer, therefore, embraces the entire Christian life, in the main aspects of it, which we may speak of as THE FUNDAMENTAL EQUIPMENT, THE PROGRESSIVE EXPERIENCE, and THE MANIFOLD EXPRESSION.

Under each of these thoughts a great wealth of truth is presented. Consider then, first—

I.—THE FUNDAMENTAL EQUIPMENT OF THE CHRISTIAN LIFE (9)

Paul prays that the Colossians, and we, 'may be filled with the knowledge of God's will in all spiritual wisdom and understanding.' Every part of this utterance is heavy with blessing.

Mark, first of all, *the pursuit of the blessing*. Paul says, 'I cease not to pray and to desire.' The 'prayer' is general; and the 'desire' is particular. We pray because we desire, and it is the expression of desire that gives point and definiteness to prayer, and so, 'Whatsoever things ye *desire* when ye *pray*, believe that ye receive them, and ye shall have them' (Mark xi. 24).

The pursuit, therefore, of this and every blessing should be *prayerful*, for we are 'to pray,' and it should be *particular*, for we are 'to desire,' and *persistent* also, for we are to 'cease not' in the exercise of both.

Prayer points to the attitude and the act; desire gives concreteness to the exercise; and perseverance in both is stimulated by past attainment and present need.

Consider, further, *the nature of the blessing*. It is spoken of as our 'being filled with the knowledge of His will,' in which at least three thoughts unite:

There is first, the thought of *revelation*, indicated by the words 'His will.'

Broadly, this means, no doubt, the whole counsel of God as made known to us in Christ.

Specifically, in the light of our context, it must mean, His will for the conduct of our lives (verse 10): the moral aspect of His will as it affects us individually.

'The will of God' is one of the greatest thoughts we can contemplate, and it is essentially the subject of all revelation, now as His predestinating will (Eph. i. 5), now as His prescribing will (Eph. i. 9), now as His providential will (Rom. i. 10), revealed, on the one hand, in the Scriptures, and, on the other hand, in Jesus Christ.

There is, further, the thought of *apprehension*. The knowledge of which Paul speaks in his Prison Prayers is not intellectual, but spiritual; not theoretical, but experimental; it is not the arrangement of truth in the mind, but the regency of it in the heart.

It is ἐπίγνωσις, the knowledge of God in Christ. And let it be observed that it is the knowledge of God's *will* that is here prayed for. Important as is the study of His essence, His attributes and His counsels, we must remember that Christianity is not a system for specula-tion, but for the regulation of life, and for that, the chief thing is an experimental knowledge of the Divine will.

We shall see in a moment how this knowledge is to be applied. Meanwhile, let us learn that 'the foundation of all Christian character and conduct is laid in the knowledge of the will of God.'

Once more, there is here the thought of *repletion*. We may and should be 'FILLED' with the knowledge of God's will.

So viewed, the knowledge is the *substance* of the fulness; but further, in that knowledge we are to be complete, and that idea points to the *measure* of our apprehension of His will.

This desire, if it is at all practical, must surely limit the knowledge to the will of God for each of us, as respects our human sanctification, a knowledge in which we may be relatively 'complete,' whereas, com-pleteness in a knowledge of the larger aspects of His will, such as His whole counsel in Christ, is not possible to any of us.

This idea of 'fulness' is characteristic of Paul, and is of oft occurrence in these Prison Epistles.

This, then, is the blessing as to its nature—we may be filled with the knowledge of God's will. That will must be known before it can be done; but, being known, it should be done, and 'he that doeth the will of God abideth for ever.'

Attention is now called to *the acquirement of the blessing*. This is to be, 'in all spiritual wisdom and understanding.' If in the previous sentence is set before us a desirable *object*, in this one is revealed the *means* of its attainment.

The Divine knowledge must be brought down into the sphere of human faculties, if it is to be of any practical value.

And so, with reference to our apprehension of God's will for us are here introduced the ideas of manner, characteristic, and thoroughness.

The manner of our acquirement of this knowledge is to be 'in wisdom and understanding.'

We do not receive Divine illumination apart from our faculties, which are the means of our apprehension, and the instruments of operation. The Spirit employs those faculties with which He has endowed us, and He expects us to use them. But what are we to understand by these terms, and how are they related to one another? It may be said that wisdom is the more general, and understanding the more specific term: wisdom gives both rise and effect to understanding.

By understanding is discerned 'the relations of different truths, the logical bearing and consequences of one's principles,' and by wisdom—which is the sum of mental excellence—is that discernment made practical.

The understanding makes every aspect of the Divine the object of study: and by wisdom practical application is made to life of all those principles which the understanding severally embraces.

One may have knowledge without understanding or wisdom, and then it is a curse; but a right apprehension and application of spiritual knowledge is the secret of true Christian life, and the effectual safeguard against error.

There is great need in these days for a well-ordered comprehension of Christian truth, without which in time of mental conflict we are bound to suffer loss. Religious sentiment will not carry us very far. There is such a thing as 'the faith,' and we should have understanding in it, and be obedient to it. By wisdom and understanding must knowledge be regulated.

It should be observed what is *the characteristic of our acquirement* of this knowledge. This is defined as 'spiritual.'

The unregenerate possess the faculties of wisdom and understanding. They may have a true system of ethics, and make very good use of it, but their wisdom and understanding are never 'spiritual.'

The characteristic of those faculties in exercise in the Christian is that both are inspired by the Divine Spirit, Who, making known to us the will of God, enables us to discern its true significance for ourselves and then, to make a right application of it in practical life.

In this way wisdom in the believer is distinguished from 'the wisdom of the world,' 'fleshly wisdom,' 'the wisdom of men,' and 'the wisdom of this age.'

The thoroughness of our acquirement of this knowledge is indicated by the word 'all,' by which is meant 'every kind' of spiritual wisdom and understanding.

We are not to be satisfied with some display of 'wisdom and understanding,' but these are to be brought to bear in all circumstances, under all conditions, and at all times, and are richly to be manifested in us all, in every case as needed.

Now bring these two clauses together and we see how vitally related are creed and conduct, knowledge and action, apprehension and application.

The knowledge of the Divine will is not for its own sake, but that it might become mightily operative in the life.

Knowledge is in order to action, and 'no revelation from God has accomplished its purpose when a man has simply understood it.' 'If ye *know* these things, happy are ye if ye *do* them.' All doctrines bear on practice. The principles of truth are the laws of life.

Knowledge that does not shape conduct is relatively worthless, no matter how sound it may be; and action which does not spring from spiritual knowledge can never be spiritually fruitful. 'Morality has a basis which makes it vigorous and permanent only when it rests upon the knowledge of God's will.'

But where is that will to be found? Where must we turn for a knowledge of it? Assuredly to the Holy Scriptures in which that will articulates. The will of God is revealed in the Word of God, and to be known that Word must be studied by the child of God, whose faith in it must be simple and strong, his meditation in it constant, and his obedience to it glad and complete.

This, then, is the Fundamental Equipment of the Christian life. But equipment is qualification. For what is the knowledge of God's will imparted? And for what end is it received?

This leads to the second part of the Prayer, which treats of

II.—THE PROGRESSIVE EXPERIENCE OF THE CHRISTIAN LIFE (10a)

We are to be 'filled with the knowledge of God's will

in all spiritual wisdom and understanding,' so as 'to walk worthily of the Lord unto all pleasing.'

Looking at the main thought still for a moment, let us remember that the experience is not the equipment, neither is it in order to it, but is the outcome and expression of it.

Quite a wrong place can be given to experience, and quite a false significance attached to it.

Experience is not the touchstone of truth, but truth is the test of experience.

If experience were, as some claim, the final test, then every man would be a law unto himself. But Christian experience must arise out of and must rest upon the Christian revelation.

In the first instance it is knowledge that leads to action, and not action that is productive of knowledge, though in a very real sense these have a reciprocal force. We are to be 'filled with the knowledge of God's will' in order that 'we may walk worthily of the Lord.'

All true action must spring from knowledge; worthy conduct from a sound creed; Christian ethics from Christian doctrine; right doing from right thinking; morality from theology.

Let us now examine the terms of this clause. With reference to the progressive experience, mark its practical energy; its lofty standard; and its ideal aim.

Its practical energy is revealed in the words, 'that ye may walk.'

The Christian life is described by various attitudes and actions. We are to 'sit still'; to 'stand fast'; to 'run the race'; to 'walk worthily'; and each of these ideas has its own value in its setting.

In the Prison Epistles our life is characterised as a

'walk in good works,' 'walk worthily of the vocation,' 'walk in love,' 'walk as children of light,' 'walk circumspectly,' 'walk in Him,' 'walk in widsom,' 'walk worthily of the Lord.' This metaphor is designed to give prominence to several important features of the Christian calling. For instance, *to walk implies effort*. It is not the contemplative, but the active aspect of our life that is here in view; there is a putting forth of energy; truth stirs to activity. Divine knowledge leaves no man stationary.

To walk also implies progress. Not only is there motion, but motion forward. There can be a great deal of movement without progress. However rapid the movement, there can be no advance in a circle. The Christian life is essentially a progressive life.

Furthermore, *to walk implies steadiness*. We recall the words 'they shall mount up with wings as eagles, they shall run and not be weary, they shall walk and not faint.'

The thought here does not fall but rises; it is more difficult to run than to fly, and more difficult to walk than to run. Walking implies maturity, persistence, steadiness.

For this practical energy of the Christian life, is raised *a lofty standard*. It is to be a walk 'worthily of the Lord.'

This expression sets before us a standard of conduct, and points to a level of life. It strikes the key-note of our calling. We shall not easily apprehend the significance of this word, and never in this estate fully realize the ideal.

Where, then, are we to look for *the motive of such a life?*

The Apostle answers, to the 'Lord,' meaning Christ. He says, in effect, that if life is to be lived as it may and should be, the Lord Jesus must be the constant Object of our contemplation. Writing to Timothy, he says, 'Remember Jesus Christ'; and to the Hebrews: 'Consider Jesus.'

We should consider what He is in Himself, the mystery and glory of His Person, Who is very God of very God, and truly perfect Man; and what He is in the manifoldness of His Office, Who is at once our Saviour and Priest, and Advocate, and King; and as we thus contemplate Him we shall be furnished with a motive worthy and strong to live the life set before us.

We should also consider what He has done for us. Never must we allow ourselves to forget His deep humiliation, His temptations and tears, His sorrows and sufferings, His atoning death, His triumphant resurrection, His present ministry, and His inspiring promise to come again.

As the wonder of all this breaks afresh upon our souls we shall say with new meaning, 'Love so amazing, so Divine, demands my soul, my life, my all.'

'Nothing short of complete self-surrender, perfect obedience, and unwavering, unfaltering love can characterize the walk that corresponds with our profound obligations to Him.'

Nothing within or around us has significance or power enough to move us to so exalted a life, but the Lord Jesus Christ *can* and *does*.

The manner of such a life is reflected in the word 'worthily'. Paul is fond of this word. Our manner of life is to be lived worthily of the Gospel; we are to walk worthily of our vocation, and of God; we are to act worthily of the saints; and here, 'to walk worthily of the Lord.'

In all these passages is the idea of a standard to which the practical life is to be conformed; the idea of what is becoming and fit; of what is worthy of Him Whose Name we bear. We are called to live a life which shall do honour to God, impossible of realization as it may seem.

This word is designed not to dis-spirit us, but to rouse us to a consciousness of the unspeakable grandeur of our calling. We may well ask how we can walk 'worthily' of His holiness, His glory, and His love! Yet, if we are led to aspire to such a standard, it is because it may surely be reached. God's commands are His enablings; His precepts imply promises.

If it is right that we should so live, it must be possible, incredible as it may seem. The actual in our experience is never to be the standard or measure of the possible.

We are to 'forget the things which are behind, and to reach forward unto the things which are before.'

If this lofty standard is progressively to be reached by us, it will only be as our life is governed by highest principle, and characterized by noblest performance; only as the human is pervaded by the Divine; as the temporal is dominated by the spiritual; and as the transient is touched by the eternal.

The ideal aim of such a walk is declared to be 'unto all pleasing.' The Apostle has not yet finished his definition of the Christian life. He has spoken of its practical energy, and its lofty standard; he now calls attention to its ideal aim.

The final object of knowledge, and of a Godly life, is to please God.

We should, therefore, understand what is *the significance of this aim*. The word 'pleasing' does not occur again in the New Testament, but its use elsewhere shows how unworthy may be the aim. It requires highest motive and worthiest object to preserve it from every trace of obsequiousness and grovelling complaisance, and such object and motive the Christian has.

There is here no suggestion of temporising or compromising in order to ingratiate oneself with the rich or the mighty, but rather a loving anticipation of our Saviour's will.

To 'please' Christ is to live a life in such deep fellowship with Him that our walk is characterized by an eagerness to explore His every wish.

This introduces a tender personal element which, it has well been said, transmutes the coldness of duty into the warmth of gratitude, and throws a rosy light over the snowy summits of abstract virtue.

The exclusiveness of this aim is plainly declared. It is 'the Lord' we are to please, and the aim is safe only as He is its Object.

Paul asks, 'do I seek to please men?' and warns us against 'eye-service as men-pleasers.' He declared he spoke 'not as pleasing men, but God.'

The only 'pleasing' to which the whole life can be conformed is the consideration 'how we ought to walk and to please God.'

The temptation to win the approbation of men is ever present, and generally strong, and when a man yields to it he immediately impairs his sincerity and his usefulness.

The praise of men is not at all costs to be courted,

nor their blame at all costs to be shunned. Their dis-
approval may be the signal of our triumph, and their
laudation but the advertisement of our defeat.

'There is no thought which will so reduce the importance of the babble around us, and teach us such
brave and wholesome contempt for popular applause,
and all the strife of tongues, as the constant habit of
trying to act as ever in our great Taskmaster's
eye.'

'We should labour,' then, that 'we may be well-
pleasing to Him,' remembering ever that He did always
those things which were pleasing in His Father's sight.
He, thus, is at once our example and our strength.

The comprehensiveness of this aim is also here in view.
It is to be unto '*all* pleasing.' This means that we are
so to walk as to please Him in all things, at all times,
and to the limit of an increasing ability. 'There is a
daring completeness in the sentence "unto all well-
pleasing." There is no reservation for human infirmity,
no undertone of deprecation of the Divine severity, no
hint of a tolerant construction of our conduct in the
forbearance of our Lord.'

How practical the energy of the Christian life! How
lofty the standard! How ideal the aim! We may be
pardoned if with the first burst of the truth we feel it all
to be impossible. Yet, if it be right it must be possible.
What, then, are the evidences of such a life? This is the
subject of the third part of the Prayer.

III.—The Manifold Expression of the Christian Life (10b-12)

These verses are a detailed definition of what should
characterize a walk which is worthy of Christ.

These characteristics are set forth in three participial phrases which introduce the several divisions of this part of the Prayer. These are: 'bearing fruit and increasing' (10b); 'being empowered' (11); and 'giving thanks' (12).

Thus, the outward expression of the Christian life is to-manward, in service (10b); the inward expression is to-selfward, in character (11); and the upward expression is to-Godward, in gratitude (12). Each of these clauses is laden with truth most precious.

Look at THE OUTWARD EXPRESSION WHICH IS TO-MANWARD, IN SERVICE. And, first of all, we have *the definition of our service* presented in the striking phrase, 'Bearing fruit in work.' This word occurs in verse 6, with reference to the Gospel message, as here, with reference to those who receive it; and the words are apparently taken over from our Lord's parable of the Sower, where we read that the seed in 'good ground' '*beareth fruit* and bringeth forth'; and, also, that it 'sprang up and *increased*' (Matt. xiii. 23, Mark iv. 8).

In the New Testament '*fruit*' almost always points to *character*, and '*works*' to *service*; and so, in the ninefold 'fruit of the Spirit' in Gal. v. 22, 23, there is no reference to Christian service; but here, the 'works' are the 'fruits,' the outcome of a life lived in conformity to the will of God 'unto all pleasing.'

The worthy walk will be manifested in an activity rich in productiveness. Effective service springs from true consecration.

Perhaps the consecration is suggested by the verb, 'bearing fruit,' and the service by the substantive, 'good work.'

The range of our activity is expressed as in 'every good

work.' The idea of completeness must surely arrest our attention.

The tree of life within us will bring forth, not 'twelve manner of fruits' simply, but all the fruits that the infinite diversity of the circumstances of life permit.

Our character within, and service without, are to be all-round and multiform. We are to make widely different forms of goodness our own, and if this be a Divine aspiration, it must be possible of actual experience. Nor is that all. There is to be at the same time the development of our capacity. This is conveyed by the word 'increasing.'

Some read the text as 'Bearing fruit in every good work, and increasing in the knowledge of God,' thus making two distinct clauses.

But it is better to read, 'In every good work bearing fruit and increasing.' This interpretation is warranted by the conjunction of these words in verse 6. There, 'fruit-bearing' describes the inner working of the Gospel, and 'increasing' describes its outward extension. So here, the thought is that while we are showing the fruits of our faith before men, we ourselves are, meanwhile, growing in moral stature, our own nature becoming larger and stronger.

The fruitfulness of the tree does not exclude its growth, and so we, ministering to others, are also enriching ourselves—bearing and growing, growing and bearing; and this as the expression of a 'walk' which is the product of a knowledge of God's will for us.

Thus, no limit is set to the on-going of the Christian life, to our spiritual advancement. 'The tree is for ever bearing fruit, for the secret life that feeds it knows no limit to its development; it is that of which our Lord said, "I am come that they might have life, and that they might have it more abundantly." And the life is always adding to its sum of good works; they may fill every moment, make every circumstance of the day contribute, and stamp their character upon the most evanescent movement of the soul.'

Furthermore, this passage reveals *the means of our fruitfulness and growth*. It is '*by* the knowledge of God.'

The text may be read in two ways: as meaning either that the knowledge of God is the *sphere* in which the growth enjoined is to be realised; or that this knowledge is the *instrument* or *means* of fruitfulness and growth.

The reference in verse 9 to our being 'filled with the knowledge of His will' makes it more natural to regard the 'knowledge' here as *instrumental*.

In this view it will be, as Lightfoot says, 'the dew or the rain which nourishes the growth of the plant.' But both ideas are true: knowledge affects growth, and growth increases knowledge. If we know we should do (Jno. xiii. 17), and as we do we shall know (vii. 17). As we bring our creed into practice, our obedience will mean increase of light.

Again, THE INWARD EXPRESSION OF THE CHRISTIAN LIFE IS TO-SELFWARD, IN CHARACTER.

'With all power being empowered, according to the might of His glory, unto all patience and longsuffering with joy.'

How amazing an utterance! Mark here, the *gracious provision for our life*. We are to be 'with all power empowered.'

Great is our need of 'power,' for great is our weakness,

but God, without Whom we can do nothing, has promised us power.

We are made strong *in* the element of His strength, as we are made strong *by means of it.*

And 'all' needed power is communicated to us as all His power is ever at our disposal. The tense expresses the continual application of it. The thought also is present that He gives to us 'every kind of strength' and many kinds of strength we need in our so varied life. We may therefore know 'what is the exceeding greatness of His power to-usward who believe.'

See also, what is *the Divine proportion* for our life. It is, 'according to the strength of His glory.' The 'glory' of God is the splendour of His Self-revelation in which now one, and now another, attribute is given prominence.

Here, the attribute of His glorious majesty brought out is His 'strength,' because our immediate need is of power.

The 'strength' of this all-glorious God is the source and standard of our power supply, and is ever exercised on our behalf. The strength given knows no limit on His part, and is limited on ours only by our capacity and faith.

This, then, is 'the immeasurable measure of the strength which may be ours.' Our capacity is at each moment the working limit of the measure of the strength given us. But it is always shifting, and may be continually increasing. The only real limit is 'the might of His glory, the limitless omnipotence of the Self-revealing God.'

We look again, and learn what is *the enriching pro-*

duct of such a life. It will be 'unto all patience and longsuffering with joy.'

How arresting a sequence! We would scarcely have been astonished to read that we needed to be empowered with the Divine strength for strenuous service and heroic deeds, but it is surprising to learn that we need power for gentleness: not for 'a rush of energies a torrent of witness, a blaze of miracles, a life which is to "make history" in the world's sense of the words,' but 'unto all patience and longsuffering with joy.'

This impartation on His part, and reception on ours of all kinds of power according to the strength of His glory, is in order to the practice of passive virtues!

And what are these? 'Patience and long-suffering.'

Patience refers to our attitude to trials; but long-suffering to our attitude to persons.

Patience is endurance of what is imposed; but long-suffering is resistance of the temptation to rebel.

Patience is stout-heartedness under ill-fortune; but longsuffering is magnanimity under ill-treatment.

Patience is the opposite of cowardice or despondency; but longsuffering is the opposite of wrath or revenge.

Patience is closely allied to hope; but longsuffering is closely allied to mercy.

Patience is fortitude in oneself; but longsuffering is forbearance with others.

Patience is well illustrated in Job as hopeful endurance, and longsuffering is perfectly illustrated by Jesus in His bearing the insults of His enemies.

For this end are we strengthened and in this way are we enriched.

The Divine power is not at our disposal for selfish aggressiveness or for proud exploitation of ourselves;

but, on the contrary, for the manifestation of meekness and mercy.

There is promised us the giant's strength, but not, as the poet says, to use it like a giant.

It might be thought that the cultivation of these virtues would be productive of gloominess and moroseness, and so the Apostle adds 'with joy.' He does not say 'unto' joy, as though it were to be the product of patience and longsuffering, but 'with joy.'

The joy accompanies the struggle; it is, so to speak, engendered by it. The very conflict itself is joyous; and the consciousness of triumph ever brings its own exultation. Ours is to be joyful fortitude and joyful forbearance; our clouds are to be rimmed with flashing gold, and we are to sing our songs in the night.

And finally, THE UPWARD EXPRESSION OF THE CHRISTIAN LIFE IS TO-GODWARD, IN GRATITUDE. 'Giving thanks unto the Father.'

The final expression of such a life is praise. Here the Apostle's devotion passes into doctrine, and the prayer goes off into infinity; but on the way he would have us know that *the reason for thanksgiving* is 'the inheritance provided for the saints'; that *the sphere of the blessing* is 'the light'; and that *the ground of our claim* is the qualification we have through His redeeming grace.

From this the prayer rises to the contemplation of Christ as the First-born of every creature, the Creator and Sustainer of all things, visible and invisible, the Head of the Body the Church, the First-born from the dead, and the Fulness of God. All the Divine fulness is in Christ, and all of Christ is for us. If we are impoverished we are impoverished in ourselves. We are the true millionaires, we are the inheritors of wealth incalculable, we are the possessors of all that is worth having in heaven and in earth, in time and in eternity.

Let us rise to a true sense of our calling, of our dignity, of the grandeur of our destiny, and, Spirit-filled and Christ-driven, let us go forth and give the message of His redeeming love to all mankind. That is our high and solemn commission, and I pray God we may not fail of it.

Wherefore I also, after I heard of your faith in the Lord Jesus, and love unto all the saints,

Cease not to give thanks for you, making mention of you in my prayers;

That the God of our Lord Jesus Christ, the Father of glory, may give unto you the spirit of wisdom and revelation in the knowledge of him:

The eyes of your understanding being enlightened; that ye may know what is the hope of his calling, and what the riches of the glory of his inheritance in the saints,

And what is the exceeding greatness of his power to us-ward who believe, according to the working of his mighty power,

Which he wrought in Christ, when he raised him from the dead, and set *him* at his own right hand in the heavenly *places*,

Far above all principality, and power, and might, and dominion, and every name that is named, not only in this world, but also in that which is to come:

And hath put all *things* under his feet, and gave him *to be* the head over all *things* to the church,

Which is his body, the fulness of him that filleth all in all.

Ephesians 1:15-23

3

PRAYER FOR SPIRITUAL ILLUMINATION

WE shall divide the prayer of Eph. i. 15-23 into three parts: considering first, the Occasion of it (15, 16); secondly, the Object of it (17-19); and finally, the Outlook of it (19-23).

First of all, then—

I.—THE OCCASION OF THE PRAYER (15-16)

This we see to be threefold. To begin with, it was prompted by the amazing change wrought and manifest in these Ephesians. The Church was composed of Jews and Gentiles who had been converted to God, but the Gentile converts are throughout more especially in view.

The Apostle, both before and after this prayer, remembers, and reminds them of their past state by nature and their present standing by grace. They were without Christ, but they are in Christ; they were afar off but now they are nigh; they were strangers, but now they are citizens; they were foreigners, but now they are sons; they were branded by sin, but now they are sealed by the Spirit.

As the Apostle thinks of all this he uses two expressions profound with significance: 'but now' (ii. 13), and 'but God' (ii. 4); words which reverse their preceding state and experience. 'Wherefore,' for this cause, he prays.

The second thing which moved him to prayer was

the report to hand of their present spiritual
condition.

If the thought of their position in Christ leads him
to the Throne, so does the news which he has received
of their condition of soul. We should distinguish
between position and condition in this connection,
between the judicial and the experimental. In true
Christian life the latter will be approximating ever
more nearly to the former; we shall be becoming what
we are.

Then, maintaining, as almost certainly should be
done, the Authorized Text, news has reached Paul of
his converts' faith in the Lord Jesus, and love unto all
the saints. Every word here is weighty with significance.
Let us look at them in pairs.

There is first, Faith and Love. These stand to one
another in the relation of cause to effect, of centre to
circumference, of root to fruit, of fountain to stream, or
of principle to action. These God has joined together
and we may not put them asunder.

Then, there are the prepositions: 'in' and 'unto,'
the one conveying the idea of fixity, and the other the
idea of flow; the one pointing to the sphere of their
faith, and the other pointing to the object of their love;
the one signifying location, and the other direction.

Then, mark that, their Faith is in the Lord Jesus,
that is, in the God-Man; for 'Lord' points to His Deity,
and 'Jesus' to His Humanity, and both are united in
the 'Christ' of verse 17, so that only the Lord Jesus Christ
can be the foundation and object of saving faith.

Further, the Apostle says that their love is unto all
the saints. The believer's love is to be catholic and not
restricted. He loves God, of course; but he is to love

the saints also; not some of them only—which would
be easy; but all of them always—which is very difficult.
'If we love not our brothers whom we have seen, how
can we love God Whom we have not seen?' (1 John
iv. 20).

The true test of a Church's prosperity is not the
number of members it can claim, not its financial wealth
and material plant, not its social status and weight of
prestige, not its multiplied activities and variety of
interests, but its spiritual progress; and the essential
elements in this are growing faith in Christ, and deep-
ening love for one another.

In proportion to the strength of our faith and the
richness of our love, will be the brightness of our hope
(18).

But once more, this Prayer was occasioned by the
Apostle's unceasing joy and hope on their account. The
joy finds its expression in thanksgiving, for he says, 'I
cease not to give thanks for you'; and the hope finds its
expression in intercession, for he continues, 'making
mention of you in my prayers.' Both these activities
meet in prayer.

Thanksgiving is retrospective, but intercession is
prospective; thanksgiving is for the foundation already
laid, but intercession is for the superstructure going up;
thanksgiving is for past attainments, but intercession is
for future advancements; thanksgiving is for the actual
in their experience, but intercession is for the possible in
God's purpose for them.

By thoughts so rich and full is the Apostle drawn out
in prayer for his beloved converts among whom he
lived and laboured so long. If this be but the approach

to his intercession for them, how great must be the intercession itself. So, let us now turn to—

II.—The Object of the Prayer (17-19a)

This is preparative (17-18a), and progressive (18b-19a), the dividing lines being indicated by the conjunction in verse 17 (ἵνα), meaning, in order that; and the preposition in verse 18 (εἰς) meaning, with a view to. The first paragraph points to a process and the second to a product.

Let us look first of all at the Preparative Object (17-18a). The central idea here is that a blessing in the way of a 'gift', is offered to us, and the source, the nature, and the condition of it are set forth.

The *Source* of the blessing is, 'the God of our Lord Jesus Christ, the Father of glory.' The expression, 'Father of glory,' may mean simply, that from above comes every manifestation of the Divine presence in the world; or, that He is the Author of glory; or, that He is the Bestower of glory; or, that to Him glory characteristically belongs.

But it may easily mean more. If, remembering that the Shekinah of old was 'the symbol of the Divine residence in humanity through the incarnation of the Son,' we take 'glory' here to mean the Divine essence in Christ, then the first expression, 'the God of our Lord Jesus Christ' would point to a relation derived from Christ's human nature; and the second expression, 'the Father of glory,' to a relation derived from His Divine nature.

This was the view of Athanasius, and if the passage before us does not definitely say this, it at least holds the suggestion.

As to its nature, the blessing is 'the Spirit of wisdom and revelation in the full-knowledge of Him.' This gift is set forth as to the medium, the elements, and the sphere of it.

We learn that the *Medium* of the blessing is 'the Spirit.' The terms employed do not permit of our regarding 'spirit' here as man's spirit, but rather the Holy Spirit, Who is at once the Gift and the Medium of it.

He only can reveal the truth which is reflected in the word, 'revelation,' and enable us to make a right use of it, reflected in the word 'wisdom.' Thus, here, as so often in this Epistle, the three Persons of the Godhead are revealed in their relations and operations: the Father of glory, the Bestower of knowledge; the Lord Jesus Christ, the Substance of it; and the Spirit of wisdom and revelation, the Communicator of it.

Then the *Elements* of the Blessing are 'wisdom and revelation.'

Let us mark in passing that the order of experience is the reverse of the order of the text. But what do these terms mean, and how are they related? It may be said that the revelation is objective, and the wisdom subjective; the revelation is related to truth, and the wisdom to life. The revelation makes the wisdom possible, and the wisdom makes the revelation practical.

The 'Spirit of revelation' functions in two ways—as the Spirit of inspiration, in the Scriptures now complete; and as the Spirit of interpretation, in the Church continuously. But if revelation is to bring good to us, and glory to God, it must articulate in wisdom. Heavenly principles must find practical expression; the truth must become operative. For this reason we have the con-

junction here of revelation and wisdom, and these must
not be put asunder.

Here, also, we learn that the Sphere of the Blessing
is 'in the knowledge of Him.' The revelation is not of
things in general, but of Christ; and the wisdom is not
the apprehension and application of truth in general,
but of evangelical truth; and so, the knowledge of
God in Christ is the scope and sphere of the blessing
here prayed for. This is further confirmed by the word
for 'knowledge' here employed, ἐπίγνωσις. Its force may
be gathered by a reference to 1 Cor. xiii. 12: 'now I
know (γινώσκω) in part, but then shall I fully know
(ἐπιγινώσκω) even as I have been fully-known' (12). All
knowledge of God is γνῶσις, but the knowledge of Him
in Christ is ἐπίγνωσις. This 'full-knowledge' is not mental but experimental, not intellectual but spiritual. It
is in the field of this knowledge that the revelation is
vouchsafed, and here also has wisdom scope for its
finest display.

The blessings for which Paul prays are not temporal
but spiritual, not special to some but common to all
believers, not transitory but abiding.

And yet further, the Condition of the blessing is that
'the eyes of the heart be enlightened.' The reference is
to the state from which these converts have been de-
livered. Paul says of them, 'ye were once darkness, but
now are ye light in the Lord' (v. 8). Before their conversion they were 'darkened in their understanding'
(iv. 18), but now 'the eyes of their heart have been
enlightened,' and that makes possible to them every
other blessing.

The 'heart' is the 'inner man,' the seat and centre of
our mental and spiritual life, in which intellect, and

feeling, and will unite. In the great experience of conversion the 'eyes of the heart' are opened, and from that time forward may and should be continuously enlightened.

The force of the word is 'having been' and 'being' enlightened, pointing to an operation which is at once instantaneous and progressive. In both cases the 'enlightenment' is the condition of the blessing of 'knowledge.' Let it be understood also that the enlightenment is not the illumination but the preparation for it. The light is not the truth but the medium of it.

All that has been said up to this point is but the preparation for what is to follow. We must now turn our attention to

II.—The Object of the Prayer (18b-19a)

All the preceding is 'granted' unto us with this in view, 'that we may know . . .'

A threefold progression is clearly marked by the recurrence of the word 'what', introducing sentences singularly full and precious. Each is an advance upon the one preceding; each refers both to God and ourselves; and to each is attached the conception of looking onward.

The Spirit prepares us to know 'what' is the Brightness of the Hope imparted to us; the Fulness of the Inheritance set before us; and the Greatness of the Power exercised towards us. So weighty are these thoughts that language well nigh breaks down beneath them; and it is little wonder that expositors have variously interpreted these words.

Let us observe first of all that we are enlightened to know what is *the Brightness of the Hope* imparted to us.

How are we to understand these words? Is the 'hope' subjective, or objective? Is it the emotion or grace of 'hope' that is referred to, or the object of 'hope,' the thing hoped for? Is Paul speaking of expectation itself, or of the thing expected?

Surely where language is so ambiguous as to be fairly capable of this double construction, both ideas may be allowed. In this way how comprehensive is the prayer! It is nothing less than that we may know in happy experience the expectation which God's saving calling of us has begotten in our souls; and that we may know also what that calling has secured for us, and reserves for us in the heavenly life which awaits us.

This 'hope,' therefore, has its origin and its issue in salvation. The 'calling' from which this expectation springs is spoken of as 'His,' not as *ours*, because it is not our privilege that is here in view so much as His boundless grace. It is the 'calling' of which God is the Author, and by which this 'hope' is effected. If a choice must be made between the two possible interpretations of 'hope' in this place, it would be best, in the light of what follows, to regard it as the Christian expectation itself, rather than as the object of it, which latter seems to come into view in the next clause.

In the next place, we are enlightened to know what is *the Fulness of the Inheritance* set before us. And here again the language is ambiguous. Is the Apostle speaking of the inheritance revealed in us, or the inheritance reserved for us? Is the reference to God's inheritance in *us*, or ours in *Him*? The expression may, grammatically, be understood either way, being read as 'His inheritance in the saints'; or as 'the inheritance of which He is

Origin and Substance, and which is known and revealed among the saints.' It is easy to believe that our
inheritance in Him is rich in glory, but most difficult to
believe that He can regard us in that way. For this
reason the former view has been much insisted on.

But let not faith stumble here. In the Old Testament
the Israelites are spoken of as God's portion (Deut. iv.
20, vii. 6, Jer. x. 16, Mal. iii. 17), and in verse 11 of this
chapter *we* are spoken of as God's inheritance, 'we are
made a heritage,' and again, in verse 14, we are called
'the purchased possession,' which must mean God's
own possession of and in us.

This thought, therefore, cannot fairly be excluded
from verse 18. Almost certainly both ideas are here,
that of His inheritance in us, taken over from verses 11
and 14, and that of our inheritance in Him, taken over
from verse 14.

This double significance is confirmed by the terms in
which the inheritance is characterised, 'glory' and
'riches;' the 'glory' pointing to His manifestation in us
His portion, and the 'riches' referring to our experience
of Him our portion. His is the 'glory,' ours are the
'riches,' and each of us is the inheritance of the other.
In this view the inheritance is not wholly present, and
is not wholly future, but it is here and now entered upon,
and will there and then be fully possessed. In verse 7 we
read of 'the riches of His grace,' and here, of 'the riches
of His glory.' As certainly as the 'grace' is not limited
to time, so certainly is the 'glory' not limited to eternity.
We may know both, here and now, but the experience
of 'glory' is an advance upon the experience of 'grace.'
All believers know the latter in measure, but compara-
tively few the former.

And finally, we are enlightened to know what is *the Greatness of the Power* exercised towards us. This is the final clause in the grand progression, in each part of which are linked together 'God and the saints,' and the 'present and future.'

With reference to the former, let it be observed that it is His calling and our hope, His glory and our riches, His power and our faith. And with reference to the latter, it is hope now within us, and the object of it yet to come; inheritance now enjoyed, and yet to be fully realised; power now exercised in response to faith, and yet to be fully demonstrated at the resurrection.

Mark also in these clauses a progress of thought reaching from the commencement to the consummation of the Christian life. The expectation is the grace of Christian hope created in us at conversion; the inheritance is the object of Christian hope to be kept steadily ever before us, and the power is the guarantee of the fulfilment of Christian hope progressively and at the end.

If these wondrous truths are ever to come within the field of experimental knowledge, verily we must look to the Spirit of truth to 'enlighten the eyes of our heart.'

Furthermore, the experience of this power is conditioned on faith; it is 'to-usward who believe.' This certainly means that the power spoken of is exercised on behalf of all Christians, who are such by virtue of having believed; but the words in their context require a fuller interpretation, for although we have believed unto salvation, the Apostle prays 'that we may know the exceeding greatness of His power.' with a knowledge which is not theoretical, but experimental, and such a knowledge comes only in response to faith.

In other passages power and faith are related, as
when we read that 'our faith is to stand, not in the wisdom of men, but in the power of God'; and that 'we
are kept by the power of God through faith.'

That power is here regarded as in God surpassing all
limit, and as in us limited only by faith, faith which is
at once the condition and instrument of the operation
of the Divine strength. It is faith whereby we enter,
and take possession and rejoice.

This brings us to the third part of our study, which
really takes us beyond the prayer; for here, as in Colossians, the Apostle is, in spirit, carried into the Divine
glory and wrapt in its holy light.

So let us contemplate briefly—

III.—THE OUTLOOK OF THE PRAYER (19b-23)

How vast the outlook! There are presented to our
vision, and all in relation to our life, the Resurrection,
Exaltation, and Dominion of Christ, and these verses
constitute the climax of the prayer and the very life-
breath of our faith and love and hope. Paul is still
speaking of the Divine power, and is interpreting and
illustrating its 'exceeding greatness.' He defines it in a
way which shows again how language struggles to give
expression to Divine thought.

Three terms are used which must not be regarded
as synonymous, but as marking a definite gradation:
'operation' ($\dot{\epsilon}\nu\dot{\epsilon}\rho\gamma\epsilon\iota a$), 'strength' ($\kappa\rho\acute{a}\tau os$), and 'might'
($\dot{\iota}\sigma\chi\upsilon s$). Behind the Divine 'operation' which we see and
feel is the Divine 'strength,' and behind that strength
are the infinite resources of the Divine 'might,' and all
these unite in the display of the Divine 'power' ($\delta\acute{\upsilon}\nu a\mu\iota s$).

Let us take time to be impressed by this description

of God's power, or the tremendous force of this passage will be missed. The phrase means 'the efficiency of the active power which expresses inherent might.'

Now it is time to see how all this is brought into relation with ourselves. 'The eyes of our heart are enlightened, for us to know what is the exceeding greatness of His power to-usward who believe, according to the working of the strength of His might which He wrought (ἐνεργέω), in Christ when He raised Him from the dead.'

The revelation here is simply overwhelming. It is nothing less than this: that the operation of the exertion of the might of God, displayed in the resurrection and exaltation of Christ, is the measure of that surpassing power—the guarantee of our hope—which He puts forth to-usward who believe. The exercise and effects of the Divine power are indicated in a way designed to show the decisiveness and completeness of the successive acts.

Mark the five aorists here: He wrought in Christ; He raised Him from the dead; He seated Him in heaven, He put all things under Him; and, He gave Him to the Church.

In these clauses the prayer goes off into infinity, wherein a threefold evidence of the Divine power is set before us: First, in the *Resurrection of Christ* (19b-20a). 'He wrought in Christ when He raised Him from the dead.' Two standards of the Divine power are exhibited in the Bible. In the Old Testament it is the dividing of the Red Sea; and in the New Testament, the resurrection of Jesus Christ. It is the historical fact of Christ's resurrection that is here referred to, and this is declared to have been wrought for Him, not merely as an individual member of the race, but as the representative of His people.

The resurrection of Christ is the supreme exhibition of the Divine power, and it carries with it also the resurrection of His people, *now* to newness of life, and *ultimately* to bodily glory.

Thus, in Phil. iii. 10, Paul desires that he may know the power of Christ's resurrection, and looks on to the time when 'Christ shall change our body of humiliation that it may be fashioned like unto His body of glory' (21).

The exercise of this Divine power is limited only by our faith; it is to-usward 'who believe.'

The standard of His operation should be the standard of our expectation, and, to the limit of growing capacity, the standard also of our experience.

The power of God is further revealed in *the Exaltation of Christ* (20b). 'He seated Him on His right hand.' This utterance is as pregnant as it is brief. There is here the thought of rest, 'He seated Him.'

The place God appointed Him He occupied, and, if the anthropomorphism may be allowed, there He *sits* in token that His work is finished. 'When He had by Himself purged our sins, He sat down.'

Also, we see here that the 'right hand' is the place of distinction and privilege, and the 'left hand' is next unto it. For this reason James and John wished these places in relation to Christ in His kingdom. But it is declared that God, by the exercise of His might, has given to Christ the highest place in the universe in relation to the Throne. This is His indisputable right.

And this introduces the thought of glory, 'in the heavenlies.' This expression must mean 'in heaven,' the idea of locality being reflected in the words 'seat' and 'right hand.'

Christ has 'passed through the heavens,' and has entered 'into heaven itself,' now to appear in the presence of God for us. And this fact apprehended issues in a vision of *the Dominion of Christ* (21-23). It is still the power of God that is being illustrated. The power by which Christ was raised, He was also seated; the power by which He was raised and seated, He was given dominion; and that is the power which is 'to-usward' who believe.

In this revelation of Christ's dominion are several distinct declarations, which, together, show His supremacy to be unshared.

It is first declared that *His Dominion is over all Intelligencies* (21), 'above all Rule and Authority, and Power and Lordship.'

These expressions point, not to principles and forces, but to personal powers, classes and categories of personal beings, and that of each there are many, is indicated by the '*all*' meaning every kind of celestial intelligence.

We know little of these orders of angelic dignity and power, and of their functions, but what is most important to know is here revealed, namely, that the Christ Who was crucified on Calvary, raised by the Divine power, and seated in heaven, is '*over-above them all.*'

And not only 'above' all and every kind of these unsinning intelligences, but 'above *every name that is named.*'

Above all created objects throughout the whole universe, by whatsoever name called; and that, not only in the present age, but in all possible future ages.

The supremacy of our Christ is absolute, and the glory of His Person is matchless!

From the lowest depths of humiliation 'God exalted Him and gave Him the Name which is above every name, that in the Name of Jesus every knee should bow of things in heaven, and things in earth, and things under the earth; and that every tongue should confess that *Christ is Lord*,' and the power which God exercised upon, and transferred to Him, is that which He exercises 'towards us who believe.'

It is next affirmed that *His Dominion is over the whole Creation.* 'He put all things under His feet.'

In the preceding verse created intelligences only were in view, and all of them, but here the idea is widened to include *all created things* in heaven and in earth, rational and non-rational, organic and inorganic, visible and invisible.

Not a few passages announce this UNIVERSAL DOMINION OF CHRIST, a dominion, which, as God's gift, is already His, but which He not yet universally exercises and enjoys. And finally is revealed *His Dominion over the universal Church.*

It is little wonder that the thought here is somewhat involved, seeing that the truth is so profound. The main truths which find their common focus in this utterance are that God gave HIM, this all-glorious Christ, to the Church; that He was given to the Church in His capacity as 'Head over all things'; and that the Church is His Body, so that He is the Head of it also.

And it is further, and finally, declared that this same Christ is 'the fulness of Him Who filleth all in all.' God has given Him to the Church Who is at once Head over all things, and the embodiment and manifestation of the Divine fulness, for 'in Him dwelleth all the fulness of the Godhead bodily; and in Him we are filled full.' The future is with the Christian; the glory is before us; the brightest and best is yet to come. Governments may rush into hopeless chaos, and worlds may totter to their fall, but as certainly as the Christ of God lives, His people shall survive all wreck of matter and crash of worlds, and flourish in immortal youth. His resurrection is the type and token of our own, 'because He lives we shall live also.' Let us go forth with this magnificent vision of the dominion of our great and blessed Lord, filled with His Holy Spirit, to tell tremendously in our impact upon our generation, and so to hasten the day when 'the kingdoms of this world shall become the kingdom of our Lord, and of His Christ.'

For this cause I bow my knees unto the Father of our Lord Jesus Christ,

Of whom the whole family in heaven and earth is named,

That he would grant you, according to the riches of his glory, to be strengthened with might by his Spirit in the inner man;

That Christ may dwell in your hearts by faith; that ye, being rooted and grounded in love,

May be able to comprehend with all saints what *is* the breadth and length, and depth, and height;

And to know the love of Christ, which passeth knowledge, that ye might be filled with all the fulness of God.

Now unto him that is able to do exceeding abundantly above all that we ask or think, according to the power that worketh in us,

Unto him *be* glory in the church by Christ Jesus throughout all ages, world without end. Amen.

Ephesians 3:14-21

4

PRAYER FOR DIVINE PLENITUDE

GREAT as have been the other prayers it may not be too much to claim that this one in Eph. iii. 14-21 is the greatest, for it includes them all. There is nothing conceivable for the believer, beyond 'the fulness of God.' That brief word goes beyond all that we have ever experienced, and sums up all that we ever may experience.

The fulness of God is just God Himself as revealed in Christ and ministered by the Spirit. No larger thought can occupy our finite minds.

This is one of the great Scriptures, the Holy Spirit's words of the first order, and is, perhaps, the most fervent, comprehensive and sublime prayer in the Bible.

'What John xvii is to the Gospels, this Prayer is to St. Paul's Writings. Connecting it with the preceding Prayer (i. 15-23) we have in these two effusions the loftiest language of human worship not uttered by the Lord Himself.'

All that we can hope to do is to mark the order that reigns in this tumult of holy words.

Let us consider then, first, the Approach to Prayer (14-15), then, the Appeal for Plenitude (16-19), and finally, the Ascription of Praise (20-21). First, then,

I.—THE APPROACH TO PRAYER (14-15)

'For this cause I bow my knees unto the Father of

whom the whole family in heaven and earth is named.'

Here, we should mark, to begin with, the occasion of the prayer. 'For this cause.'

This is a resumption of the petitions which Paul began to offer in verse 1, and from which he was led into a digression on the mystery of the Church. He now returns to his previous line of thought in the same words, 'for this cause.'

At once we ask, for what cause? and for answer we must go back, if not to all that has preceded, at least to ch. ii, where the writer has drawn two pictures, one of what these Gentiles once were by nature, and one of what they now are by grace. They once were slaves, but now have the freedom of the city; they once were outcasts, but now enjoy the fellowship of the family; they once were paupers, but now are admitted to the fulness of the sanctuary.

As he brings into sharp antithesis the words 'once,' and 'but now' (ii. 13), and, 'sin,' 'but God' (ii. 4), the holy joy of his soul must find expression, and so 'for this cause' he prays.

The prayer, therefore, is the product of a double vision, first, of the poverty and need of the Ephesian believers on the one hand, and of the spiritual stores provided for them in Christ on the other hand, and it has for object the getting of the one into contact with the other.

Observe, further, the posture Paul assumes; 'I bow my knees.'

It would seem as though at this point he was so full of earnest longing and rapturous delight that he fell upon his knees as he continued to write or dictate to his amanuensis. The attitude betokens unusual emotion and is the sign of the deepest reverence and humility.

The address is 'unto the Father.'

Paul is not thinking here of God's relation to Christ, but of His relation as Father to the redeemed family, as the context shows. Because He is our Father we can come to Him with assurance; and because our Father is our God, we must ever come with adoration. Every time we say 'Our Father,' we should think of His goodness, and every time we add 'Who art in Heaven' we must think of His greatness.

He is the God of all men, but the Father of such only as believe, for it is only by the Spirit of His Son that we can cry 'Abba, Father.'

Without, therefore, bringing ourselves into bondage in prayer, it will be well to remember that our supplications should be 'towards Him' ($\pi\rho os$), for, not only in redemption, but in fellowship also, it is, 'thro' Christ that we have access by one Spirit unto the Father.'

Then, how inspiring is the outlook—'of whom the whole family in heaven and earth is named.'

The recollection of the Father opens up to the imagination of the Apostle a vast realm of spirits who have their common origin in God as Father.

Whether we read 'the whole family,' and understand the redeemed in heaven and on earth; or read, 'every family,' and understand all orders of intelligent beings, human and angelic, the point of the utterance remains the same, namely, that God is the great original and prototype of the paternal relation wherever found, and that we, through the redeeming mediation of the Son, share in the blessedness of His nature and name.

With so impressive an approach to prayer we shall

feel eager to know what holy thoughts filled the suppli-
ant's mind, and what mighty passion moved in his soul.

This is given expression to in the words that follow.

MACLAREN has well said that, 'in no part of Paul's
letters does he rise to a higher level than in his prayers,
and none of his prayers are fuller of fervour than this
wonderful series of petitions. They open out one into
the other like some majestic suite of apartments in a
great palace temple, each leading into a loftier and
more spacious hall, each drawing nearer the presence
chamber until at last we stand there.'

The great goal of the prayer is in the words (19), 'the
fulness of God.'

All that precedes prepares us for, and leads us into
this exalted experience. In this, as in the other Captivity
Prayers, human desire and thought reach their limit,
they grasp at the infinite.

But let us turn to the prayer itself, which we have
called,

II.—THE APPEAL FOR PLENITUDE (16-19)

Although all these petitions are so closely knit, and
thought melts into thought, yet, there are observable
distinct stages in the unfolding design, and, with the
Divine fulness in view throughout, our attention is
called, first of all, to the necessary preparation for it
(16-17), then, to the growing illumination in it (18-19a),
and lastly, to the final realization of it (19b).

THE NECESSARY PREPARATION FOR THE DIVINE FUL-
NESS (16, 17), is twofold, the strengthening of the Spirit,
and the indwelling of the Christ.

Twofold I have said, but these are one, and are not

separable, though perhaps this is the order in which they are to be conceived.

First, then, the Divine fulness is conditioned upon *the strengthening of the Spirit* (16). Paul prays that the Father would grant to us 'according to the riches of His glory with power to be strengthened, through His Spirit, in the inner man.' It is assumed that every spiritual blessing comes to us as a *gift* from God.

While it is the answer to a sense of want, and a spirit of dependence on our part, it is, on His part, an act of sovereign grace. We cannot purchase, and we do not merit the least of the blessings here set before us, but in answer to believing prayer, God will 'grant' them.

What it is that the Father will grant unto us is now revealed, as to its nature, agent, sphere, and measure.

The *Nature* of the blessing is, 'to be strengthened with power.'

A great degree of weakness is possible where there is life, and surely there must come to each of us with every fresh self-discovery a sense of our urgent need to be strengthened, strengthened in mind and heart and will.

In Philippians Paul prayed that we may have a Discerning Love; in Colossians, that we may know the Divine Will; in Ephesians i., that we may have the Eyes of our Heart Enlightened, and here, he prays for a blessing which, if bestowed and received, will lead to an experience and enjoyment of all the rest, namely, that we may be strengthened, and strengthened with Power.

The Apostle has spoken in the previous prayer of power; there, however, it is power as *put forth by God*, but here, it is power as *imparted to us*.

The Pentecostal promise was, not that we should receive knowledge or wisdom, or any of those many qualities and blessings of which we stand in such great need, but that we should receive power whereby every other grace will be made possible.

Both the Christian and the Church have no greater need than of power. Learning, and wealth, and prestige and organization, and far-flung activities can be no compensation for the lack of this.

The initial blessing is the inclusive one in that, if power be offered and received, it will open the way for us into all 'the fulness of God.'

And we are here reminded of the *Agent* of the blessing; it is through 'His Spirit.'

As at the beginning it is written 'ye shall receive power after that the Holy Spirit is come upon you,' so still, it is through Him alone that such 'strengthening' is possible, and by Him only is 'power' imparted.

This superhuman might of God operating in men is always referred to the Holy Spirit. He is to us first of all the Spirit of life, and ever after, the Spirit of power, the fountain of spiritual energy.

It is true that this blessing of strength by the Spirit is to be continuous and ever-increasing, but the tense (aorist) shows that it is also to be definite and decisive.

To numberless Christians who once lived in practical neglect of the Holy Spirit, this experience of Him as the imparter of power has come with all the force of a revelation. Power is given as it is needed, but there is a first reception of it which changes the whole complexion of life. Shall we not pray, even now, for this grace, and then answer our prayer by receiving it.

Attention, further, is called to the *Sphere* of the

blessing. It is 'in the inner man.' By this expression is meant our central and highest life, the noblest portion of our being, the seat of our intellectual and spiritual life with its impulses and feelings and struggles, the 'hidden man of the heart,' the rational moral self, our whole conscious personal being, in short, our true personality.

This 'inner man' in the unregenerate is darkened, being under subjection to the flesh, but when quickened by the Spirit of God it becomes the 'new man,' and the sphere of the Divine operations.

It is here, at the very core of our personality, that we need to be strengthened, in the secret springs of action in the interior man.

Into this inward man (for that is the force of the pre-position $\epsilon i\varsigma$), the strengthening is poured; 'into' or 'towards' it, as an object, this gift is directed. Our central life is the sphere and destination of the blessing vouchsafed. Nothing less than this will satisfy the Divine design, or bring us into the experience of 'the Divine fulness.'

We look again at this so pregnant passage and see what is the *Measure* of the blessing. This is declared to be 'according to the riches of His glory.' Who can measure the bountifulness of God! In all His giving He is lavish, prodigal, overflowing. His measures are measureless. He ever acts up to the dignity of His infinite perfections, which, here, are spoken of as His 'glory'. His giving is according to His rank and wealth, so that, if we are impoverished and weak, it is in ourselves, and, in view of the riches at our disposal, such a state is not only pitiful, but sinful.

This, then, is the first part of the preparation for the Divine fulness. And the second is, *the indwelling of the Christ* (19). 'That Christ may dwell in our hearts through faith.' We shall consider here, the meaning, seat, condition, and effect of this indwelling.

As to its *Meaning*, this thought marks an advance upon the former, and is really the result of it. We are 'strengthened' so that Christ may dwell in our hearts. The strengthening is granted with a view to the indwelling. But surely Christ already dwells in our hearts, for how else are we Christians? That aspect of the truth must never be lost sight of, for He most surely is in us except we be reprobates. And yet that is not the whole of the truth. He Who is here may yet come, and come more richly and fully.

It is well said that His presence in us has its degrees and advances, its less and more, its outer and inner. A life may be truly Christian and yet far from being fully Christian. It is this which distinguishes one Christian from another. Some have made little room for Christ, some give Him more, and in some He has the whole house. Or, viewed from another standpoint, in some Christ is just present, in others He is prominent, and in others again, He is pre-eminent.

We have never received so much of Him as to render this passage meaningless for experience. Fresh revelations of Himself are ever awaiting us, and new impartations of Himself are ever possible. He may be in us as Saviour, and not as Lord, as mighty Redeemer, yet not as Friend. We may be conscious of His presence and yet, lamentably ignorant of His power.

It is for the indwelling of 'the' Christ for which Paul prays, that is, 'Christ in the significance of His name,

Christ not only possessed but understood; Christ real-
ized in the import of His work, in the light of His re-
lationship to the Father and the Spirit, and to men.'
Christ would dwell in our hearts in the same way in
which the Divine fulness dwells in Christ (Col. ii. 9).
He would find in us, not a precarious habitation, but,
a fixed dwelling place, a permanent home.

And this leads us to observe the *Seat* of this indwelling
It is 'in your hearts.' The 'heart' is the centre of feeling,
and thinking, and willing, our interior conscious self,
the central chamber of the soul, the very shrine in the
temple. And it is in our 'hearts' that we are to sanctify
Christ as Lord.

This means vastly more than an intellectual, or philo-
sophical, or theological apprehension of Christ. We
may have all that, without having this. Christ may be
in our heads without being in our hearts. We may hold
the truth about Him without being held by Him the
Truth. For this latter we need to be 'strengthened'
so that He may 'dwell in our hearts,' for if He be there,
He will be everywhere, but He may be otherwhere
without being there.

How, then, is this experience to become ours?
There is now revealed the *Condition* of this indwelling.
'Through faith.' The blessing of an indwelling Christ
is, on one side, the effect of Divine operation, but, it is,
on the other side, the result of human apprehension
and appropriation. Faith is the hand that opens the
door for this blessed incoming, it is the instrument by
which the possible becomes the actual, and no other
faculty can do its work.

The Divine promises are made to faith, not to intellect. The reception of Christ to the very core of our

being is neither mediate nor theological, but experimental, that is to say, it is neither mechanical, nor
intellectual, but spiritual.

Faith is more than exalted aspiration, it is 'an
affirmation and an act that bids eternal truth be fact.'
The incoming of Christ to the heart in this rich way
is not inevitable, it must be (as the tense indicates)
critical and decisive. Faith must begin to appropriate
Christ, and that beginning will carry with it the secret
and promise of all that is to follow.

One more thought remains, namely, the *Effect* of
this indwelling. Before the Apostle announces the end
for which the Spirit's strengthening and Christ's indwelling are the necessary conditions and preparation,
he indicates what the effect will be of that double
blessing.

In doing so he uses two figures and both in relation to
the Divine love. That love is the *soil* in which our life
must have its roots, and it is the *rock* on which our faith
must ever rest. So Paul speaks of our being 'rooted and
founded,' setting forth the Christian life as at once a
tree and a temple. Both figures convey the ideas of
security and stability.

The perfect participles convey a double truth,
namely, that this state is the outcome of the strengthening and the indwelling, and that it is the necessary
condition of the 'apprehension' and 'knowledge' of
the following clauses.

Let us not lose the thread of thought in the multi-
plicity of details. So far the prayer has shown what is
necessary preparation for the experience of 'the fulness
of God.'

This, we have seen, is twofold; the strengthening

of the Spirit, and the indwelling of the Christ, which together will have for their immediate result our establishment *in* and *on* the love of God, and the experience of that love as the constant principle of our life.

From such preparation the Apostle goes on to speak of THE GROWING ILLUMINATION IN THE DIVINE FULNESS (18-19a).

All that has preceded is in order that 'we may be fully able to apprehend with all the saints what is the breadth and length and depth and height, and to know the love of Christ which passeth knowledge.' This paragraph circles round the verbs 'to apprehend,' and 'to know,' which must not be regarded as synonymous.

First of all, therefore, Paul prays that, as an outcome of the Divine strengthening and indwelling we may have ability to 'apprehend.' We say 'apprehend' rather than 'comprehend' as more suited to finite faculties. The idea is of a mental grasp of the thing set before us, yet a grasp, which, while ever increasing, can never be inclusive or exhaustive. Our being 'fully-able' to apprehend means that all the time we may do so to the limit of a growing capacity.

And now we must ask what it is that we are to apprehend, and how we are to apprehend it. In answer to the first inquiry the Apostle says 'What is the breadth, and length, and depth, and height. The sentence is unfinished, and this has led to much conjecture as to the object in view.

Is Paul thinking of the dimensions of the Church, the Temple of God, of which he has already spoken in this Epistle? If so, he sees that Church ideally as spread through all the world, as having its origin in a past eternity, as raised out of the dark quarries of sin and misery, and as destined through all eternity to be a habitation of God through the Spirit.

Or is Paul thinking of God's redeeming plan for the world? Then he sees it to be all-inclusive, and everlasting, and radical, and effective. But as the Apostle has just spoken of love, and is about to speak of it again, perhaps it is more natural to supply the genitive 'of the Divine love.' The connection would then be that we being rooted and founded in *love* may be fully-able, with all saints, to apprehend that *love* in all its dimensions and in our individual experience to know the *love* of Christ which passeth knowledge.

No doubt, in using this rhetorical language Paul's one idea was simply to set forth the surpassing magnitude of God's love for us. Yet it is entirely permissible for us to see here distinct ideas which in combination constitute the wonder of that love.

The breadth of His love tells of its *extent*. It is a love inclusive, comprehensive, universal. It embraces all nations, and reaches from pole to pole. 'God so loved the *world* that He gave.' 'I, if I be lifted up from the earth will draw all men unto me.' The redeemed of the Patmos vision are 'a great multitude of all nations.'

The length of His love tells of its *duration*. It is a love unoriginated, age-abiding, everlasting, from eternity to eternity, without beginning, pause or end. 'I have loved thee with an *everlasting* love.'

The depth of His love tells of its *condescension*. It is a love unprovoked, unrestrained, and untiring, reaching to the lowest abysses of sin and misery. It is the love of the 'Hound of Heaven,' chasing us out of all our hiding places. It is 'His great love wherewith He loved us,' so that each may say, 'He loved me and gave Himself for me.'

And finally, the height of His love tells of its *transcendence*. It is a love, lofty, sublime, and infinite. Depth and height are one dimension, so that the depth of His humiliation for our redemption, is the measure of the glory to which He will lift us in the day of His final triumph. His love is of immeasurable measure, and of boundless bounds, who can know it!

It was a truly spiritual conceit that led an early writer to find in these dimensions an allusion to the shape of the Cross, for there the Divine love was consummated, and there we must look if we would see its most moving display.

> See from His head, His hands, His feet
> Sorrow and love flow mingled down.
> Did e'er such love and sorrow meet,
> Or thorns compose so rich a crown?

We may now ask how such a love as this is to be apprehended. The answer is twofold, namely, individually and collectively. The individual aspect is emphasised in the next verse, but the collective aspect in this verse. When the Apostle says, 'with all the saints,' he affirms that apprehension is possible only to saints.

> The love of Jesus, what it is
> None but His loved ones know.

But this expression means also, that it takes all the saints of all the ages worthily to apprehend the love of God in Christ. There is a bracing catholicity about this passage. No one age, or church, or soul has any monopoly of the love Divine, nor can we afford to act as though we were independent of one another. Infinite blessing is the common inheritance.

This is the true knowledge of the saints, and this study is the common and open privilege. No individual or group of individuals can apprehend the Divine love except in infinitesimal measure, therefore the wider our fellowship the firmer and fuller will be our hold of the love of Christ. 'The measures of the Divine purpose are indeed beyond the comprehension of any individual intelligence; but in union 'with all the saints' we may be able to comprehend them. Each saint may grasp some portion; and the whole of the saints, when we all "come to the perfect man," may know as a whole, what must for ever transcend the knowledge of the isolated individual.'

Paul now passes from what is general to what is more particular and prays that we may have also ability to 'know.' The apprehension is general, and the knowledge is particular; the apprehension is more historical, and the knowledge is more experimental; the apprehension is social, and the knowledge is personal. The advance is from without to within.

Apprehension of the measures of the love of Christ as displayed in redemption is not enough, we must know that love as a personal possession, and ever more intimately as our capacity increases.

We should know it with a knowledge that is spiritual and experimental, and must never be discouraged by the fact that 'it passeth knowledge.' This divine object invites our observation and pursuit and yet at every step outreaches our comprehension; leading us on, yet never allowing us finally to arrive.

> It passeth knowledge that dear love of Thine,
> My Jesus, Saviour; yet this soul of mine
> Would of Thy love in all its breadth and length,
> Its height and depth and everlasting strength
>   Know more and more.

From this we are led to THE FINAL REALIZATION OF THE DIVINE FULNESS (19b), for which there have been the necessary preparation and a growing apprehension. 'We may be filled unto all the fulness of God.'

We can now consider this amazing conception only in summary. It is nothing less than *infinite blessing and blessedness* that is set before us.

As to the Nature of it, what is offered is 'the fulness of God,' all the excellence that is in God, the whole glorious total of what God is.

As to the Possibility of it, the Spirit says: 'ye may be filled,' now, continuously, and for ever. All the fulness of God is in Christ, and all the fulness of Christ is for us (Col. ii. 9-10).

As to the Measure of it, it is εἰς, which may be translated as with, or into, or unto. If as 'with,' then this 'fulness' will be the *substance* with which we are filled; if as 'into,' then it will be the *element* into which we are filled; and if as 'unto,' then it will be the *goal* which is set before us, our eternal destiny.

The second and third thoughts are certainly here with all the wealth of truth which they imply.

And finally, as to the Condition of it, we must again think through all this prayer.

By the strengthening of the Spirit Christ will come to dwell more largely and richly in our hearts, and this double blessing will result in a fuller apprehension and knowledge of the love of God in Christ, and all

this will have for its issue our being ever more com-
pletely 'filled into the fulness of God' as a vessel into
the ocean, and 'unto' it as the end and crown of all
our hopes.

How great a possibility and how bright a prospect!
Well may the prayer at this point melt into

III.—THE ASCRIPTION OF PRAISE (20-21)

Just when we are thinking how utterly impossible
of realization all this is, the Spirit says, 'now unto Him
Who is able to do,' to do what we ask, to do what we
think, to do all that we ask or think, to do above all
that we ask or think, to do exceeding abundantly
above all that we ask or think 'according to the power
that worketh in us.'

Is this too much to hope for, to ask, to take? Not so
long as He is in the question, Who is Himself the
Pleroma of God. He is the present, abiding and all-
satisfying secret.

> Through the meadows, past the cities, still the brimming
>   streams are roll'd,
> Now in torrent, now expanding into silver lakes and gold,
> Wafting life and increase with them, wealth and beauty
>   manifold.
> Whence descends the ceaseless fulness, ever giving, never dry?
> Yonder o'er the climbing forest, see the shining cause on high,
> Mountain snows their watery treasures pouring everlastingly.

Yes, our unfailing Cause is shining there on high,
'to Whom be glory in the Church and in Christ Jesus
unto all the generations of the age of the ages.' Amen.